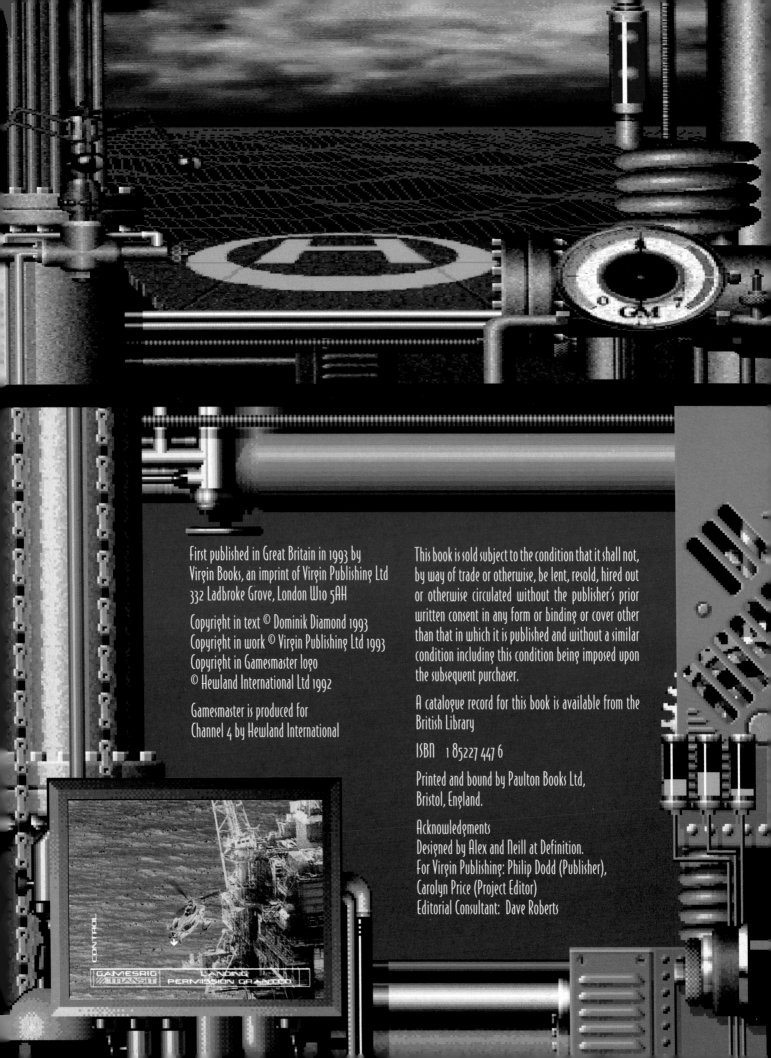

First published in Great Britain in 1993 by
Virgin Books, an imprint of Virgin Publishing Ltd
332 Ladbroke Grove, London W10 5AH

Gamesmaster is produced for
Channel 4 by Hewland International

A catalogue record for this book is available from the
British Library

ISBN   1 85227 447 6

Printed and bound by Paulton Books Ltd,
Bristol, England.

Acknowledgments
Designed by Alex and Neill at Definition.
For Virgin Publishing: Philip Dodd (Publisher),
Carolyn Price (Project Editor)
Editorial Consultant: Dave Roberts

GAMESMASTER™

THE OFFICIAL BOOK

The insider's guide to the Gamesmaster universe

IN ASSOCIATION WITH
CHANNEL FOUR TELEVISION

CONTENTS

Welcome, dear reader.
Welcome to the Book of the Show of the Legend.

I, of course, am the Legend.

You, however, can call me GAMESMASTER — or at least you could if I ever let my standards slip far enough to allow you on to the Gamesmaster Show

No doubt your slow but enthusiastic mind is wondering just what lies in-store for you over the next few pages.

Well, one excellent idea that leaps to the front of my quite brilliant mind is for you to read the thing and find out. But as I've been asked to waste precious nano-seconds of my time providing you with an introduction, I suppose a few clues are in order.

Basically, what we have prepared for your delight is a selection of the best of the last series of GAMESMASTER plus a whole host of extras.

There's a lot of waffling from that buffoon Derek Diamond (or whatever his name is), banging on about his close showbiz pals, all of whom I had to promise auto-graphs just to get them to be civil to him. Thankfully there is also quite a bit from me including the best tips from the show to guide you sadly lacking young 'uns through some of your favourite Sega, Nintendo and Amiga games. There's a quiz to determine whether or not you qualify as a GAMESMASTER; have a go if you need further confirmation of your inadequacies.

Against my better judgement I have also permitted the inclusion of a special Gamesmaster trivia quiz, the winner of which will be invited to come along and join the audience for the filming of one of the Gamesmaster shows and also gets the exciting opportunity of meeting me.

Right, that's enough of my pearls cast before you swine. My time is precious and I still have to perfect. My disembodied state suffered a shock with the explosion of the Rig at the end of Gamesmaster II, not least at the thought of being lumbered with all the work without that Diamond boy to help out, but I have been granted an unsuspecting sidekick who will bring you up-to-date. Turn the page and get clued-up.

Enjoy...

GAMESMASTER 111

DEXTER FLETCHER reporting for duty. Not for the first time, GAMES-MASTER has taken the lead, leaving everyone else wallowing in his wake.

It was the government who finally called us in. They had to admit that the crisis was getting too big for them to handle. Let's be honest, they just didn't understand what was going on.

The way they looked at it, the nation was swarming with video gamers, totally out of control. It was threatening their plan for a controllable population. You don't see too many Mega Drives down at Henley.

The way GAMESMASTER looked at it, the powers that be had missed the point. Video gaming was just completely outside their realm of comprehension.

So we suggested founding the GAMESMASTER ACADEMY OF EXCELLENCE. And we've made it happen. It's the hardest academy to join, it's open only to the top gamers around, and we have the toughest ever entry qualifications. But if you make it here, you'll know you're up there with the very, very best.

The men in suits fell for it. They thought this was a neat way of controlling all those unruly gamers. They even gave us a fortress as a base. They think we're going to fall in line. They couldn't be more wrong.

When I arrived, I really didn't have much to go on. The briefing was minimal. The only documents left from the smouldering wreckage of the Rig were jottings from Dominik Diamond and some charred sheets of scribbled notes which the Gamesmaster had down-loaded to him.

These are those notes - we've learnt everything we can from them.

Let me tell you straight - you'll need to extract as much information as possible if you're going to have a hope in hell of making it into the Academy.

I'll leave you to it. And expect you to watch us diligently.

nine

★★★ GAMESMASTER'S HALL OF GAME FAME ★★★

TOP TEN ALL-TIME GREATS

③ BODY BLOWS
AMiGA

The best beat-'em-up on the Amiga. OK, so it's a copy of STREETFIGHTER, but it's streets better than the Amiga version of it.

ten

CHOOSE YOUR FIGHTER

① STREETFIGHTER 2: TURBO EDiTiON
SUPER NES

Astounding that a console can produce games this fast. Now it can, it begs the question whether we'll ever see a beat-'em-up that's this good again.

② MORTAL KOMBAT
MEGA DRiVE

Just as in the arcade category, this game has the runners-up spot. The game plays best on the Mega Drive, because Nintendo removed all the blood and guts from their versions. Boo!

④ FiNAL FiGHT CD
MEGA CD

The first game on the Mega CD that was good and showed that if we can get perfect arcade conversions like this happening in the future, CD may be worth the money.

ACTiON GAMES

FLASHBACK
MEGA DRiVE

The ads for this said 'the first CD game in a cartridge' which is probably true. They used a new graphics technique called 'rotoscoping' which gave true cartoon-quality graphics. Worth persevering with this one!

PiLOTWiNGS
SUPER NES

A truly original game, making the most of the Super NES's mode 7 graphics chip. You pilot planes, hang-gliders, jet packs and parachutes and generally have a great laugh.

PiNBALL FANTASiES
AMiGA

Again, a really original game. Four cracking tables complete with bumpers, ramps, hidden bonuses and tilt. But, f you go 'tilt crazy', then the tables freeze up!

THE CHAOS ENGiNE
AMiGA

Almost all of the Bitmap Brothers games are classics. This one took the 'Gauntlet'-type maze shooting game and set in a weird 'techno-victorian' setting. It oozes class from every pore, allegedly.

iK+
AMiGA

Probably the oldest game featured in this special line-up, but listen, you would not even be dreaming of STREETFIGHTER 2 if this hadn't come along. The first classic beat-'em-up, this great karate game featured three-player action. Still good to play today.

STAR WARS
NES

A console game with a difference. For a start it's one of the few film tie-ins that have been any good. Secondly, this was rock hard. Few players complete the game.

STAR RIGGERS: 1

As everyone knows, there are few Shows celebs are more desperate to appear on than GAMESMASTER.

Flowers, credit card numbers, even bit parts in West End musicals - they've all been offered in an attempt to have a chance of grabbing a Golden Joystick.

How do we choose them? Only those who pass our sternest muster are filed away on Gamesmaster's cyber-network celeb-file.

These are previously unreleased extracts from Dominik's assessments, run through his Domometer™ for gamesplaying skillls and how nice they really were.

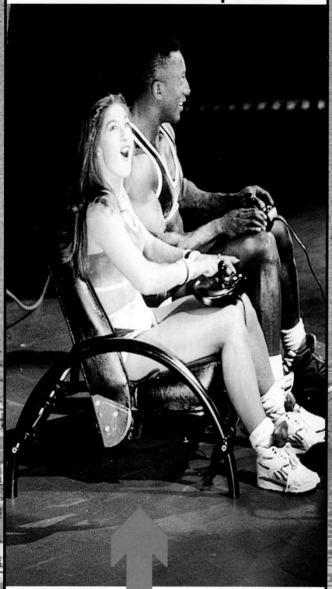

thirteen

THE GLADIATORS

Two of the Gladiators have appeared on the show; 'Yes, he's harder then me and I'm not going to argue' Shadow; and 'Every young boy's pin-up' Jet. They took part in a head-to-head race on the AMERICAN GLADIATORS Mega Drive game, which has yet to be released in the UK. It was more a test of wrist power than mental matter and it was Shadow who emerged as the easy winner, with Jet getting into all sorts of bother on the bicycle pulleys. But then life's like that.

GAMESPLAYING SKILLS **
PERSONAL NICENESS ****

EAST 17

These four young scamps came onto the Rig all the way from the wrong side of the tracks in Walthamstow. The boys played SUPER PROBOTECTOR on the Super NES, a game which is particularly tough, so they each had one life to complete the first level. Like Take That, there was a marked division in gamesplaying skill, with Brian and Tony being zapped in quick succession, John doing a bit better, and Terry being nigh-on outstanding. They didn't win the challenge, but Terry at least got one of Auntie Marisia's cakes as a consolation prize. Can't complain.

GAMESPLAYING SKILLS
****(Terry) ***(John)
*(The others)
PERSONAL NICENESS ***

THE LEGEND OF THE

GAMESMASTER™

The most asked question in television is undoubtedly,
'Just who is that Gamesmaster bloke'.
It's a difficult one to answer, because, to be frank, nobody
really knows. However, now and again, when he hits some of
Auntie Marisia's cooking sherry, he starts rambling about the old
days and this is what I've managed to piece together.

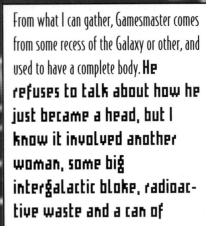

From what I can gather, Gamesmaster comes
from some recess of the Galaxy or other, and
used to have a complete body. **He
refuses to talk about how he
just became a head, but I
know it involved another
woman, some big
intergalactic bloke, radioac-
tive waste and a can of
WD40.** He was a bit of a dashing young
blade, was Gamesmaster, and I think he
messed with the wrong people, and as a
result of his 'accident', the big man is not
fond of violence.

One night, I was lying asleep in bed in my little house in the little fishing town of Arbroath, Scotland, when a face appeared
to me in a dream, well, actually, it was more of a nightmare, because this face had a huge, bulbous, metallic domehead,
which obviously took several tins of brasso and a small army of cleaners to polish. **The face had one normal
eye, and one which was enormous, and covered by a monocle. The face was
surrounded by all kinds of machinery, which popped in and out at regular inter-
vals.** Then the face spoke: **'Greetings, young Diamond, I have travelled through space
and time, turning off at Junction 4 of the M25 to reach you. We are at the beginning of a new era of televisual excitement, featuring the new "Young People"
craze: video games. I am the Gamesmaster - you will be my Spokesman.'** A centre
forward for CELTIC FC perhaps, but never a spokesman for a bulbous-headed mutoid from God knows where. 'How much do
I get paid'? I asked. And so it began.

After he lost his body, walking around was generally a bit of a problem, as I'm sure you can imagine. Just being a head, meant that he lost his place in the local darts team, and didn't pass his driving test. He had always dabbled in computers, though, and found out a way to leave behind the physical world with all it's pain and heartache and transform himself into electrical waves. So, basically, he **'Lives' in a weird kind of alternative world, and can move instantly through anything electrical. Remember that, next time you're making a bit of toast.**

While he was zipping around the inner universe, he hit upon the idea of Video Games. This was the only world he could move around freely in, so there was no better being than him to become the ULTIMATE GAMESMASTER. He immersed himself in this phenomenon, studying every aspect of it for over a century, breaking their world record on space invaders in the process. **At this point in time, it is physically and mentally impossible for anyone to ever know more than he does.** In spite of all these powers, he's never managed to grow another body, but nobody's perfect.

There are some people who think that all the years spent in electronic cyberspace have somewhat frazzled the old bloke's mental matter: in short, that he's a couple of fire buttons short of a joystick. I have never seen any proof of this, other than his unhealthy hatred of seagulls, which he took to blasting with a machine-gun halfway through the last series. You may think this is a little eccentric, but when you bear in mind the mess they made of his helmet, and the fact that he has no hands to wipe it with – I'm sure you can understand.

Despite his lonely existence in cyberspace, Gamesmaster still gets human urges like you and I, and these urges have never been stronger than in the case of his undisguised passion for Auntie Marisia. He is the one man who has seen through the blancmange and soufflés to the real woman beneath, though I must confess I do find the whole thing embarrassing. At his age gallivanting around like a young teenager is really not on, especially where my Auntie is concerned.

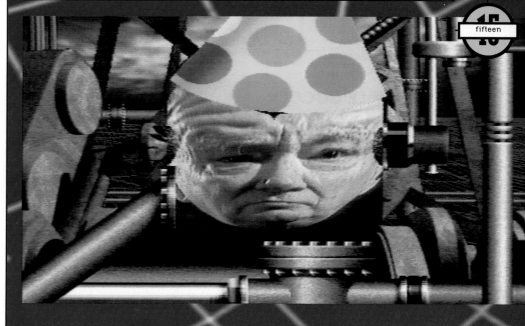

Perhaps, as time goes by, we'll come to learn more about the Great Man. Where's he really from? What are his ambitions? Does he drive a cyberspace Lada? What's his favourite flavour of crisps? Hopefully, one day these and many more questions will be answered. Or maybe not.

TOP TEN ALL-TiME GREATS

③
SUPER TENNIS
SUPER NES

Possibly the greatest two-player game of all time, I've seen some extraordinary tactics adopted in the hope of beating the opponent.

PITTS '78 AT SAN FRAN '84

CHAMPIONSHIP

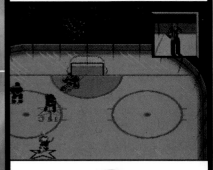

①
SENSiBLE SOCCER
92/93
AMiGA

The greatest computer version of the greatest sport. Simple as that. This game is so playable and so classy, that we even requested that they put a GAMESMASTER team in it. Which they did on later versions.

②
JOHN MADDEN '93
MEGA DRiVE

I'm sure nobody in the UK cared about American Football before this game came along. Since the Madden series began, there's been many imitators, but none of them have come close enough to do up the laces of this one.

④
NHLPA HOCKEY
MEGA DRiVE

Hockey is a great stress reliever - tripping, kicking and punching is allowed in this gripping ice-hockey competition.

SPORTS GAMES

⑤ PGA TOUR GOLF 2
MEGA DRIVE

In this classic golf game, they have this brilliant option called a 'skins' game, where each hole is worth money to the winner. Why not substitute the money for pints of tizer for added pressure!

⑥ GOAL !
AMIGA

Before SENSIBLE SOCCER came along, the KICK OFF games were the business. This latest in the series, however, while not measuring up to the playability of SENSIBLE, is a good runner-up.

⑦ ROAD RASH 2
MEGA DRIVE

A driving game with the bonus of added violence and the head to head option make this one of the fastest sports games as you fight it out over the baking-hot tarmac.

⑧ SPEEDBALL 2
AMIGA

This probably remains the greatest Bitmap Brothers game. The fact that it is the oldest game in the Hall of Sports Game Fame is proof that this futuristic cross between football and basketball was ahead of its time.

⑨ WORLD LEAGUE BASKETBALL
SUPER NES

Basketball games have never been that successful in the UK, because they've been a bit monotonous. This one uses mind-blowing 3D graphics to really create the atmosphere.

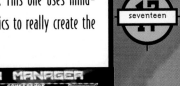

⑩ PREMIER MANAGER
AMIGA

A lot of football management games are terribly serious, complicated and slow. This is quite a simple affair, with the result that anyone can pick it up quickly and rattle through a whole season in a few hours.

GAMESMASTER'S CONSOLETATION ZONE
SEGA™

Right, listen up, pay attention and you might just learn something. Being blessed with a brain the size of a planet, I don't find video games a problem or even much of a challenge. But then I don't find time travel and alchemy that taxing.

I do understand, however, that some of you painfully limited young scamps do have trouble completing Sega games.

Naturally, in your times of gaming crisis you turn to me. Well, to cut down on the amount of my precious time that your elementary questions waste, I've decided to gather together some of your more common queries and match them up with my complete and perfect answers.

So, prepare to be impressed...

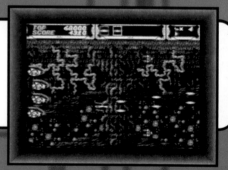

1. **'I'm finding THUNDERFORCE 3 very difficult. Can you make it any easier for me?'**

'During play, pause the game and then press the following combination on your control pad: Up ten times, B twice, Down twice, B six times and A once. When you unpause the game you will be equipped with the full arsenal of weapons.'

© Disney

2. **'Where are the secret levels in MICKEY MOUSE'S CASTLE OF ILLUSION?'**

'From the start, go through the middle door. After you've met the first clown don't go up the ladder. Instead, pick up the block and throw it near the toy train. You should now be able to jump on the cloud of smoke from where you will be able to access a hidden level.'

3. '**I can't seem to get enough power in to my kicks in EUROPEAN CLUB SOCCER. What should I be doing?'**

'Go to the password screen and enter the word 'THREE' on the first line, 'SHREDDED' on the second line and 'WHEAT' on the third. You will now be blessed with shots of awesome power.'

4. '**Is there an invincibility cheat on JAMES POND 2: ROBOCOD?'**

'There is indeed. As soon as the game starts, walk right until you see the Artic Toys sign. Above the board you will see a number of objects which you should collect in the following order: Cake, Hammer, Earth, Apple, Tap. The first letters of these objects collected in that order spell the word 'CHEAT' and you are now totally invincible.'

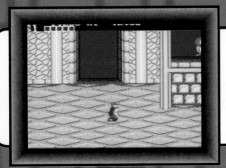

5. 'On DOUBLE DRAGON on the Master System, is there a way of getting infinite lives?'

'Play through to the fourth level, go into the middle of the screen and do two back kick leaps. Repeat this move until 'PUSH START' appears. You now have infinite lives.'

6. 'On POPULOUS on the Mega Drive, is there a cheat to take me to any of the levels?'

'When entering the level code, enter the number of the level and then the word 'BIT'.'

7.'Is there a way of making ECCO THE DOLPHIN any easier?'

'How about becoming invincible? That should help. Go to the password screen and enter the code for the level you wish to start on. But before exiting the screen, press A and then Start. Keep them held down until the game begins. If you release them, the game should pause. Press Start again and you are into the game but totally invincible.'

THE DIVER

Age: 25 Hair: ? Eyes: ?
Fave Game: Ecco the Dolphin

There are fewer tales in television more tear-jerking than that of the Diver who presents the Golden Joysticks on GAMESMASTER. At one stage, the Diver was an international model known enigmatically as 'Whiska'. She was at the pinnacle of her career, hanging out with Naomi Campbell, Kate Moss and all the other super models , refusing to get out of bed for less then $10000 when everything went tragically wrong. She was modelling the latest in underwater wear off the coast of Scotland, when a nuclear explosion occurred in the depths of the sea.

The diving suit she was wearing was fused onto her skin, which is why you never see her without her diving outfit on. Battered and near unconscious, she doggy-paddled her way to a nearby oil-rig, which is where I found her. I offered her a job as my personal assistant, and she split her time between helping me and fighting crime anywhere she was needed.

GAMESMASTER'S PORTRAIT GALLERY

Who were they? Where are they now? Dominik Diamond gives the low-down on his friends that were

AUNTIE MARISIA

Age: It's impolite to ask
Hair: Distinguished grey
Eyes: Still sparkling with the joys of youth
Fave Game: King of the Monsters

Seamen the world over know there are few places they will receive a warmer welcome than in Auntie Marisia's Boudoir, where her beef pie has warmed many a cockle over the past millennium. Auntie Marisia used to be head chef at SPAGO'S in Los Angeles, where she served up many an appetizing *hors d'oeuvre* to the likes of Stallone, Schwarzenneger and the grumpy bloke from ONE FOOT IN THE GRAVE. However, she felt she was getting away from the solid type of home-cooking that really made her happy. When I

offered her the post of Canteen Officer on the Rig, she jumped at the chance. Unfortunately, in the kitchen Auntie Marisia is a demon, and sometimes her 'Experiments' go awry. giving rise to the suspicion that she might have been responsible for the Rig blowing up at the end of the last series. Bless her.

THE MONK

Age: 70
Eyes: Hooded
Hair: None
Fave Game: The Secret of Monkey Island

Back when we first leapt onto the television screen, we were living in an old church in Eastern Europe. All the monks had been evacuated during the Second World War, except one. We stumbled upon him one day, deep in the bowels of the Crypt, where he had devoted himself to the study of fine teas and their medicinal purposes. Many an evening was spent with the two of us discussing the benefits of drinking lapsang suchong for sufferers of smelly feet, and it was a sad day indeed when the Monk announced he had to leave us to travel to the Far East and study under the great Tea Master, Louis Leaf. I heard a rumour recently that he's given it up and taken a job as a Marketing Director for the Milk Board, but I've seen no proof.

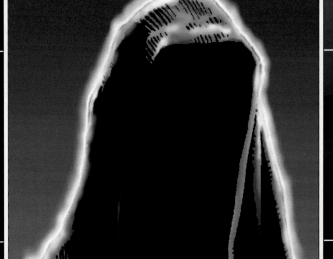

TOP TEN
ALL-TiME GREATS

③

SHiNiNG FORCE
MEGA DRiVE

The sequel to SHINING IN THE DARKNESS is not the fastest-moving game but, compulsive to play.

①

LEGENDS OF
VALOUR
PC

This is one enormous game. Initially, you don't even have a quest, you just have to survive in a town. People who live in Swindon will know this is not easy, and this game really is more of a soap opera than an adventure. Top stuff.

②

THE LEGEND OF
ZELDA
SUPER NES

AARGH!! CUTENESS!! Despite that, this is the most compelling role playing game around. Not very hard, but guaranteed to give that homework a gentle nudge away from your mind!

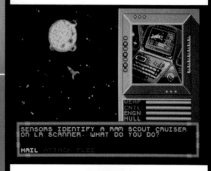

SENSORS IDENTIFY A RAM SCOUT CRUISER ON LR SCANNER. WHAT DO YOU DO?
HAIL ATTACK FLEE

④

BUCK ROGERS
MEGA DRiVE

The Mega Drive is the tops when it comes to role-playing games. Battle your way to supremacy of the Galaxy with the ever-poular space hero and his warriors,

FANTASY GAMES

THE SECRET OF MONKEY ISLAND 2
AMIGA

A game which has a spitting competition gets the go-ahead for the Hall of Game Fame. A great adventure game with plenty of laughs makes this an all-time favourite.

RINGS OF POWER
MEGA DRIVE

When this was released, a lot of reviewers panned it. This is because it is very hard and enormous in size. You really have to play this RPG for five to six hours to get into it. When you do, it's stunning. But kiss away the weekend.

CRYSTAL WARRIORS
GAME GEAR

The first real role playing game on a handheld has a real SHINING FORCE feel to it. In fact, when you get into it, it's less of an RPG and more a war-game with smart tactical battles ahoy. If you like that kind of thing.

ZELDA 2: ADVENTURE OF LINK
NES

Not much you can say that the title doesn't tell you. There's never been a Zelda game that's less then excellent. This is bigger than the first one, and it all fits onto the little NES. Isn't life great?

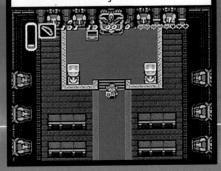

ying.....   Might and Magic: Clouds

MIGHT & MAGIC: CLOUDS OF XEEN
PC

In the ocean of RPG's for the PC, this is a blossoming island full of gently wafting palm trees and bounty bars. Could it be the easy to use interface, the gorgeous animated graphics, the snazzy speech, or the fact that it's a tough game that makes gamers come back for more?

INDIANA JONES & THE FATE OF ATLANTIS - PC

Many people prefer this to the Monkey Island games. The graphics are slightly better, the game is a bit harder, but it's not as funny and Indy's stubble is not as pronounced ! Still, If you haven't got this, people will probably point at you and call you a 'fool'.

You may have sat at home every weekend thinking 'I could do better than that guy' or 'I can't believe that girl is as rubbish as that', but have you ever SERIOUSLY wondered if you have what it takes to be a GAMESMASTER CHALLENGER? Well, if you follow the steps below, you will be swallowing the baroque atmosphere of the world's greatest games show in next to no time. Unless, that is, you don't make the grade, in which case there's always THE KYRPTON FACTOR.

JUST FOLLOW THESE STEPS:

1. LEARN HOW TO WRITE

Learning how to write is a course which is freely available at most schools in this fine country. They accept students from the age of around five. You can pretty much grasp the basics within a year, but, for those that are interested, you can carry on learning to write up to the age of 17, at which point if you are hell-bent on writing, you can go to a place called university where you meet lots of interesting people, talk about how to save the world and...er...write some more. For the purposes of beccomming a challenger on GAMESMASTER, it is only necessary to do the first few years of the course.

2. PRACTISE AT VIDEO GAMES

Unfortunately, this is not something that you can study at school, and any attempts to do so will be met with forced removal of your GAMEBOY from your hands. However, this is something you can do at home, at any time of the day, and all you need is to blackmail your parents into spending lots of money on a games machine and some games for you. And some sticking plasters for your blistered fingers.

3. WRITE AN INTERESTING LETTER

Begin with the words 'DEAR SIRS' or 'DEAR GAMESMASTER' and then BLURT EVERYTHING OUT! We want to know everything about you, including your name (helpful), address (essential), and what games your good at and what your scores are on them and, most important of all, anything interesting about yourself. This is CRUCIAL. Lots of people are really good at games, but most of them are sad, boring vegetables. We want people with something to say, who have bizzare hobbies, five year plans to get this Country back on its feet, ideas to save the planet and such-like. Anybody can complete STREETFIGHTER 2, but very few can come up with the wit and repartee demanded from a show like GAMESMASTER. That way, if you fail the challenge, we can still have a laugh!

4. ENCLOSE A PHOTOGRAPH

VERY IMPORTANT. We want to see what you look like. If you're incredibly GOOD-LOOKING, then people will watch the show and think 'Gosh! That show must be really cool if they get good-looking blokes/girls like that on it.' Some big Hollywoood producer may just happen to watch that night and snap you up to be the next box-office star. Alternatively, if you're UGLY that's even better, as it makes me look HANDSOME.

5. COME DOWN FOR AN AUDITION

If you get this far, you've done extremely well. The bad news is you have to come all the way down to our offices in London; the good news is you get to meet the people behind the scenes of TV's greatest extravaganza. When you arrive you'll get a complimentary cup of tea or coffee (you have to pay for the second one) and then you sit down and play a couple of games and have a chat. REMEMBER, the chat is probably even MORE important than the game you're playing , so, even if you whip round SUPER MARIO KART at world record-breaking pace, if you're mumbling one-word answers as you do it - you'll NEVER get on the show, BE CONFIDENT, BE LOUD, EVEN BE REALLY COCKY - we like that in a person, it makes it funny if you fail! The auditions are very informal, and the best thing to do is relax and enjoy your day. If you don't get on as a challenger, you'll probably be used as a review or in the CONSOLETATION ZONE.

6. FIND YOUR WAY OUT OF LONDON

A great game in its own right. THRILL to the complicated road systems. LAUGH at the 20 mile traffic jams. ENJOY the thrill of being squashed in a tube train with 750 million people, I tell you, London is great!

7. IF YOU ARE CHOSEN TO GO ON THE SHOW

Congratulations! And...er... don't be late. and comb your hair before you come on.

Applications to: Gamesmaster Club, PO Box 91, London E14 9GT

HOW TO BE A CONTESTANT

STAR RIGGERS: 2

BOB HOLNESS

The most ...er...MATURE celebrity we've had on the Show so far, but one of the most popular, Bob is a TV legend. Most of us on the show are lifelong fans of his, and GAMESMASTER and him go way back, as far as the 18th century someone said. Bob kept us entertained in rehearsal with many an amusing yet informative anecdote about life in the Business, and the Rig was a somewhat emptier place when he flew off. However, the Amiga, is no respector of television reputation and Bob was woeful at the game, getting stuffed by his grandson. Oh well, he had a good innings.

GAMESPLAYING SKILLS *
PERSONAL NICENESS *****

THE ARMWRESTLERS

One of the strangest challenges we had was on the arm-wrestling game, ARM CHAMPS 2 , which featured the bicep-bulging talents of Rod 'Rambo' Linett, Robert 'Bad News' Brown and Tony 'The Lunatic' Duré, all champions in their respective weight divisions and living proof that to be a success in arm-wrestling, it doesn't matter how strong you are, you need a violent nickname! All three were great blokes, as it happens, but presented us with massive problems. Tony 'The Lunatic' went first, and scored infinity which means he was so strong it went off the scale. 'Fine', I thought 'he's the winner'. Unfortunately Robert 'Bad News' did the same, and so did Rod 'Rambo'. There was nothing we could do, but declare it an AWESOME triumph of man over machine and a three-way tie. It was not, as a few people have suggested, a fix. The golden joysticks are worth a fortune and we don't like giving one away, let alone three!!

GAMESPLAYING SKILLS
Immeasurable, apparently
PERSONAL NICENESS *** (despite the trouble they caused)

JOSIE LAWRENCE

The all-singing, all-dancing, multi-talented Josie was one of the big surprises on the last series of GAMESMASTER. I thought 'here we go, she's just coming on because Tony Slattery's been on'. To put it plainly, I thought she would fail miserably. She was playing MAD DOG MACREE 2 and she'd never played it before. She flew out to the Rig an hour early, and got some practice in under the watchful eye of Doug Johns, Gamesmaster's chief playtester and the bloke who comes up with most of the challenges on the Show. So I'm thinking to myself, 'this challenge won't take long, she'll lose quickly, and I'll be able to have a nice cup of tea'. Only I couldn't, because she obliterated the challenge with a masterful display of sharp shooting and walked away with a golden joystick. I didn't get my cup of tea, which was not a problem because Josie was a smashing lady.

GAMESPLAYING SKILLS ****
PERSONAL NICENESS ****

TONY DALEY

We had a lot of brilliant games players on GAMESMASTER. It was very rare, however that the celebs were brilliant. Tony Daley, the Aston Villa and England winger *par excellence* was an exception. For a start, he was wearing round Armani glasses exactly like mine, which endeared me to him immediately. His skill as a footballer soon began to shine through as he played STRIKER on the Super NES. He give us a flurry of darting runs down the wing, an orgy of crunching, ball-winning tackles and a celebration in the art of goal-scoring as he trounced his opponent 5-0 in one of the most one-sided contests ever seen on the Show. Tony was a quiet bloke by nature, but he did his talking on the pitch, Brian, and sent us all over the moon!

GAMESPLAYING SKILLS
****
PERSONAL NICENESS ***

GAMESMASTER'S CONSOLETATION ZONE

Nintendo®

Will you rapscallions ever give me some peace? Must I constantly guide you away from the great Game Overs of life and on towards The Next Level?

It seems that I must. To make your lives easier and mine a little more tolerable I have gathered together some of the more persistent problems that you present me with regarding your Nintendo games. Hopefully this will kill a great number of birds with one enormous stone.

And incidentally, should any of you horrors happen to make it onto my Show in the future and are lucky enough to be beamed into my presence, don't ask me questions like 'Can you do this..?' or 'Can you tell me that...?' Of course I jolly well can do this or tell you that. The only area of doubt is whether or not I will. So, think on, read on and do try and keep up...

1. 'On SUPER MARIO WORLD, when I'm flying around the Ghost House in the Valley of Bowser I can see a key but I can't get to it. Can it be reached?'

'Indeed it can. The opening is obviously too small to fly through so collect the P switch and return to the mystery rock. Strike the rock from beneath and a fountain of coins will magically appear. By pressing Right and Up a few times on your keypad, these coins can be guided to create a series of steps towards the key. Then, strike the P switch and the coins will change into blocks which you can ascend to reach your goal.'

2. 'In ZELDA 3, how do I defeat Ganon?'

'Light both torches in the bottom corners of the screen, then freeze Ganon with your sword. Then, shoot a silver arrow into his miserable hide. Repeat the process six times to finish him off once and for all.'

3. 'On SUPER MARIO WORLD, where is the Green Switch Palace?'

'Travel through the underground world of Donut Plains 4 and beyond the green exit pipe until you find four blocks going up in a diagonal. If you have the cape, fly above the fourth block to find the key and key hole. If you are unable to fly, collect a shell, hurl it at the fourth block and a vine will take root. Climb this to find the palace.'

4. 'Is there a way of getting more lives on FINAL FIGHT?'

'When the title screen appears press L,B and Start to access a secret options screen where you can select nine lives.'

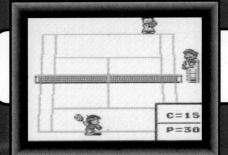

5. 'How can I beat my friend at GAMEBOY TENNIS?'

'When it is your service game, throw the ball high but instead of striking it truly, step beneath it. If the ball lands on your head, you'll have won the point without breaking sweat.'

6. 'On level 2:1 of BART VS THE SPACE MUTANTS, I can get to the floating platforms but I can't get past the spinning lollipops. What am I doing wrong?'

'Jump onto the second moving platform then jump up-and-down on it three times. You will then move automatically over the objects that are giving you so much trouble.'

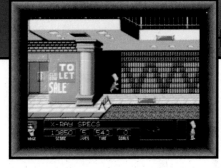

7. 'I can't kill off the guardian that hangs from the ceiling at the end of UN SQUADRON, what should I do?'

'The answer lies in the weapons that you can equip your ship with at the beginning of the level. Before you launch into the frey, buy the gun pod weapon. When you reach the end of level guardian, let rip, you'll soon have him waving the white flag.'

8. 'How do you get into the Black Hole in STARWING?'

'Flying on the easy level, go to the second stage. About half way through you will see three spinning columns with an orange asteroid in the middle. Fly directly at it but just a nano-second before you're going to collide, shoot it and fly through the debris. Do this three times. Then, an asteroid with a face will appear. Shoot at it for all you're worth and it will turn into a spinning vortex which you can fly through to enter the Black Hole.'

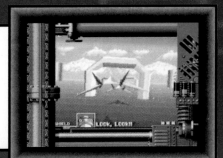

TOP TEN ALL-TiME GREATS

① SUPER MARiO LAND
SUPER NES

The classic platform game and one that has hooked many a games fanatic. It's doubtful whether we'll see a platform game as good as this again - except perhaps SUPER MARIO LAND 2!

② SUPER MARiO BROTHERS 3
NES

Despite being on 8-bit machine, this squats on most 16-bit platformers. More levels than the freemasons and much harder than them as well.

③ SUPERFROG
AMiGA

Amiga platform games have a tendency to be a bit samey. However, TEAM 17 have made a habit of doing the definitive versions of every type of game they've tried. This continues that successful habit.

④ BUBSY THE BOBCAT
SUPER NES

This almost succeeded in living up to the massive hype, and was indeed the fastest platformer to date, leaving SONIC choking in the dust.

PLATFORM GAMES

⑤ SONIC THE HEDGEHOG 2
MEGA DRIVE

You may be wondering why this is only Number 5, well for £40 it's far too easy to complete. The two player option makes up for this however.

⑥ TINY TOON
SUPER NES

This game is as cutesy and schnooky as they get. It's also very good. And it's also very hard. So after playing it for a week even I was close to cooing 'who's a pretty bunny wunny'. Or something like that.

⑦ RAINBOW ISLANDS
NES

This is the token 'oldie' in the list, a game that's appeared on just about every machine possible. It relies on the good old arcade features of short, fast levels and big, hard guardians and there are few games players who have ever completed all the levels.

⑧ ZOOL
AMIGA

This was the first time that Amiga showed it could do console-type games as good as the consoles. This was also the world's first ever masked ninja from the 'nth' dimension character!

⑨ ROLO TO THE RESCUE
MEGA DRIVE

Another horrendously cute game. What tickles my tulips about this little number is the variation given by the five different animals you can control giving this game a real puzzle element to boot.

⑩ KID CHAMELEON
MEGA DRIVE

Another game rendered brilliant by multiple characters, the only difference is that they are all within the same mixed-up kid. Yes, schizophrenia is alive and kicking in this endless game where different masks mean different attributes for the chameleon-like kid.

BEAT THE BEST

GAMESMASTER is all about challenges. Tough challenges, challenges that mere mortals would undoubtedly baulk at.

To get you wise, book purchaser type person, in on the act, I have gathered together some of the sternest tasks ever dreamed up from within this ol' ferrous head of mine. Test your gamesplaying skill by tying out the missions below.

Complete one of these and you're a bit tasty, complete more than one and you've got the right stuff. Complete them ALL and, oh dear, you obviously spend far too much time and money on video games and are in danger of becoming an insular, anti-social misfit. Try getting out more, talking to members of the opposite sex, playing football or tennis. I mean, how the hell are we ever going to win the World Cup or Wimbledon or anything with people like you sitting around...

1. - Game: Chuck Rock
Your Mission: Get through the fourth level in under 1 minute 45 seconds.
Result: ....

2. - Game: Super Mario World
Your Mission: Collect 200 coins in Donut Plains 1 and finish the stage in 1 minute 15 seconds.
Result: ....

3. - Game: Sonic 2
Your Mission: Complete Spring Yard Zone 2 and see how close you can get to the time of 40 seconds achieved by Danny Curly when he visited the Rig. Who's Danny Curly? Only the former European Sega Champion and probably the greatest mortal games player that ever lived.
Result: ....

4. - Game: Fire and Ice
Your Mission: Complete Secret Arctic Level in under 2 minutes.
Result: ....

5. - Game: The Addams Family
Your Mission: Enter the Portrait Gallery, collect 50 dollar signs, then exit within 2 minutes.
Result: ....

6. - Game: Joe & Mac - Caveman Ninja
Your Mission: Complete first level in 1 minute 30 seconds.
Result: ....

7. - Game: Sonic 2
Your Mission: Get through theChemical Plant Zone as fast as possible and see if you can match the times of our experts that played the game on the show, Paul Melerick from Mega (48 seconds) and Dean Mortlock from Sega Power (1 minute).
Result: ....

8. - Game: Super Mario World
Your Mission: Finish Chocolate Island 3 level in under 1 minute 15 seconds.
Result: ....

9. - Game: Summer Challenge
Your Mission: Give yourself three throws of the javelin and see if you can beat the distance of 87.12 metres set by the British World Record Holder, Steve Backley.
Result: ....

10. - Game: Shadow of the Beast 3
Your Mission: Complete Forest Level in 1 minute 30 seconds.
Result: ....

11. - Game: Humans
Your Mission: Complete Level One and rescue the baby dinosaur in 1 minute 30 seconds.
Result: ....

12. - Game: Tazmania
Your Mission: Complete second level of Badlands in 2 minutes
Result: ....

REVIEWS

How did these top games score on the thermometer of Gamesmaster excellency.

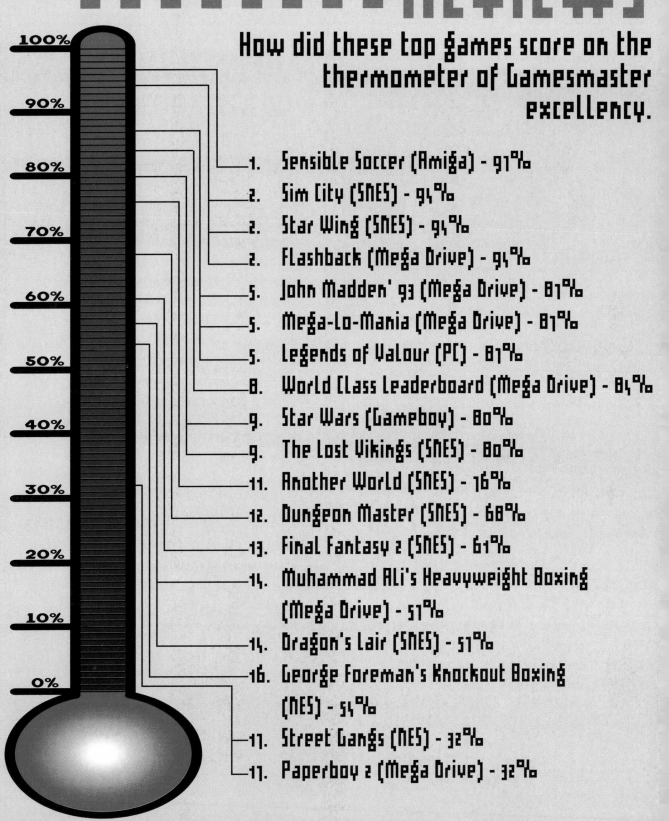

1.	Sensible Soccer (Amiga)	91%
2.	Sim City (SNES)	94%
2.	Star Wing (SNES)	94%
2.	Flashback (Mega Drive)	94%
5.	John Madden' 93 (Mega Drive)	87%
5.	Mega-Lo-Mania (Mega Drive)	87%
5.	Legends of Valour (PC)	87%
8.	World Class Leaderboard (Mega Drive)	84%
9.	Star Wars (Gameboy)	80%
9.	The Lost Vikings (SNES)	80%
11.	Another World (SNES)	76%
12.	Dungeon Master (SNES)	68%
13.	Final Fantasy 2 (SNES)	61%
14.	Muhammad Ali's Heavyweight Boxing (Mega Drive)	57%
14.	Dragon's Lair (SNES)	57%
16.	George Foreman's Knockout Boxing (NES)	54%
17.	Street Gangs (NES)	32%
17.	Paperboy 2 (Mega Drive)	32%

100%
90%
80%
70%
60%
50%
40%
30%
20%
10%
0%

STAR RIGGERS: 3

STAR RIGGERS ref: xp 249006

IAN WRIGHT

When you have one of the greatest goalscorers this country has ever produced coming on the Show to play SUPER KICK OFF, you're expecting a bit of a goal feast. Unfortunately Ian Wright, the Arsenal and England goal-machine was playing against the lovely Tammy, who plays for the Arsenal girl's team. A formidable opponent, resulting in the match being a bit of a midfield stalemate, with both teams having problems controlling the ball. The match went to penalties, and Ian's nerves began to show. He'd been quiet beforehand, and the occasion clearly got to his goalie, who was all over the shop, leaving Tammy to hoist the joystick of consummate goldness in the cause of women footballers everywhere.

GAMESPLAYING SKILLS *¹/₂
PERSONAL NICENESS ***

LINFORD CHRISTIE & COLIN JACKSON

On GAMESMASTER we try to give the viewers yummy treats at every opportunity. Well, we surpassed ourselves on the Christmas Show, when we had the first ever 100 metres meeting between Linford Christie, Colin Jackson and Carl Lewis (except is wasn't THE Carl Lewis but my, how the viewers laughed at our little name-related gag). The funny thing was, we also had a kid called Ben Johnson, who was going to appear as well but couldn't make it on the day. This show was a personal high for me, as my family have always been huge athletics fans, and I got Linford and Colin to wave to my mum LIVE on TV. Cheers! I thought Carl would cream the other two, but his time was a bit disappointing. Linford went second, and got a slow start, but stormed the second half of the race. However, Colin Jackson, who still holds the Welsh 100 metres record, ran a stormer and pipped Linford's time by a few tenths of a second. Linford demanded Colin be tested for steroids. Auntie Marisia took a sample but found nothing stronger than Lucozade. Linford was disconsolate and Colin was triumphant.

GAMESPLAYING SKILLS
*** (Linford)
*** $^3/_{10}$ of a second (Colin)
PERSONAL NICENESS infinite score
for saying 'hello' to my Mum

STAR RIGGERS ref: xp 456121

ULRIKA JOHNSON

One of the nicest experiences of my short but action-packed life was when Ulrika came out to the Rig. She was an absolute sweetheart and a BIG fan of the Show. In fact, she kept bringing up all these things from the first series that even I had forgotten. Obviously I was desperate for her to win, and in practice she was looking sharp. Unfortunately, she was taking on that most dastardly difficult of opponents, the little brother! As they began to play WORLD HEROES, all the family ties went out the window as Chris pasted his sister in the first bout. Not to be outdone, Ulrika stormed back in the second round, and we went into the commercial break facing a very tense situation. Despite a brave attempt, Chris kept Ulrika pinned in the corner as his character 'Big Mongol Bloke' knocked seven shades out of Ulrika's 'Lithe Nubile Babe' character to leave Chris with the golden joystick and me to console the fourth most beautiful woman on the planet.

GAMESPLAYING SKILLS ***
PERSONAL NICENESS ******** etc

JOHN PARROTT

There are times when I am convinced a celeb will get whipped. One such case was when we had the former WORLD SNOOKER CHAMPION John Parrott on the Rig. It was not so much that he was a bad gamesplayer, because I had no way of knowing how good he was, but more because ARCHER MACLEAN'S POOL is a very tough game, especially in a time-limit situation. Let me tell you from the start, John Parrott is a top bloke, but this would not be much good to him once the balls were racked. John's opponent scored 26 and I thought John would have no chance. However he surprised us all with a brilliant start, and then it all came down to the black into the middle pocket. If Mr Parrott potted it, he would win. He had about ten seconds left, he chalked his cue, pulled back, shot... and missed by a fraction. It was a thrilling finish, and when I pointed out to John that he'd been missing a lot of blacks in recent tournaments, we laughed in that kind of 'if we weren't on TV I'd kick your head in for saying that' way.

GAMESPLAYING SKILLS ****
PERSONAL NICENESS ****

GAMESMASTER LIVE

It was a tough life on the Rig and any break from the endless succession of chapped lips and salty seamen that plagued us all (except Gamesmaster) was always very welcome. There was, however, no more spectacular a shore-leave than when myself and the rest of the crew hopped into the surprisingly roomy Gamesmaster chopper and flew over to Birmingham's NEC for GAMESMASTER LIVE.

DOMINIK DIAMOND'S EXCLUSIVE REPORT FROM THE THREE DAY GAMESPLAYING ORGY AT BIRMINGHAM'S NEC

For those of you who don't know, Birmingham is a large city right bang in the middle of England. This heaving metropolis is famous for having a huge, complicated road intersection called SPAGETTI JUNCTION (work it out for yourselves!) and for the fact that my great Aunt Jessie lives there. Since the dawn of time it was these two factors that had attracted tourists in their millions. Well, in November of last year they had a third - GAMESMASTER LIVE!

So, by now you're wondering, what in the name of the Lord was I actually doing all this time. I know what your thinking, that I just swanned around, babes on each arm, drinking free tizer, making deals and being treated like royalty. I wish. Every day I had to put up with over 20,000 screaming punters with only one thing on their mind. To be picked to come up on our specially-constructed portable Rig set to take part in a live version of everybody's favourite show.

The basic idea was to do a computer games show to end all computer games shows. Sure, in the past they had been OK, but they'd lacked that 'skin ruffling entertainment with real pizzas' type of feeling you can only get from the crumbs at the bottom of a packet of dry-roasted peanuts...or from the greatest television show in the history of the world!

One of the best things about GAMESMASTER LIVE! was that many of the games companies there tried to do something a bit special. US GOLD, as well as having all their new games, had a mini-rollercoaster installed. Again, much to my regret, my mother wrote me a note to say that on no account was I to be allowed to hurtle round and round at breakneck speeds. So, unfortunately, I had to miss the dubious delights of that particular adventure. The same went for the flight and racing simulators and VIRGIN GAMES'S special QUASAR booth. I missed them all.

The main motivation behind their burning desire, of course, was to meet the man himself, Gamesmaster, resplendent in a perfect mock-up of the Gamesrig that we liked to call home and waited on as ever by some bloke in a stupid red jacket that I like to call Me.

Our metal mickey taker has always been keen to meet as many of you, the great unwashed, as possible and his endless patience and natural *joie-de-vivre* was in full effect at the NEC as he chatted for hours and happily signed autograph after autograph, for as long as there were eager young things waiting for a moment with their hero.

Anyway even if ol' grumpy guts wasn't exactly in party mood, he still summoned up enough enthusiasm to preside over challenge after challenge featuring punter after punter and what a strange group of gamers you were.

The Gamesmaster was certainly surprised at the huge difference in expertise demonstrated by our on-stage guests. Some of you knew your way around the leading games forwards, backwards, sideways and oops-upside-your-head, but others, it has to be said, thought a sprite was a lemon and lime drink and a RAM expansion something that only a female sheep should get excited about.

Still everyone was given a fair crack of the whip and I feel supremely confident in saying that at the end of the day, like characters on the last page of an Enid Blyton book, we were all tired but happy.

TOP TEN ALL-TIME GREATS

③ THUNDERFORCE 4
MEGA DRIVE

The definitive scrolling shoot-'em-up. The preceding game was perhaps a little too easy, this one more than makes up for it. Despite the massive amount of 'aliens with an evil posture' on screen, the game is still fast.

① X-WING
PC

The Star Wars games are the winners in this category. This is simply the best game ever that involves shooting things. Everything from the film dogfight battles are there, right down to the screech of the tie-fighters as they fly overhead.

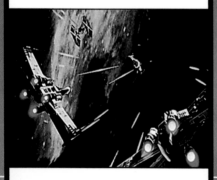

② SMASH TV
SUPER NES

A perfect conversion of the arcade classic. Complete with cheesy gameshow host, who yells 'Big Money - I Love It', and is flanked by two buxom babes. Blistered fingers or your money back with this one.

④ JUNGLE STRIKE
MEGA DRIVE

Putting the dodgy politics of the game aside, this is another original game which is also very tough. In addition to your trusty helicopter, this sequel tests your skills at piloting speedboats, jet-planes and mo-torbikes.

SHOOT 'EM UPS

5
DESERT STRIKE
AMiGA

The predecessor to the above game. It's just a helicopter this time, but the Amiga version is a bit special, with revamped graphics and much better sound then its console counterparts.

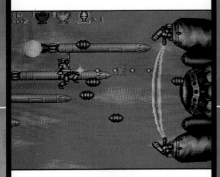

6
SUPER PROBOTECTOR
SUPER NES

One of the toughest games around. So, If you're after a challenge, this mix of sidekicks and birdseye view scrolling shoot-'em-up is the works.

7
HELLFiRE
MEGA DRiVE

The Mega Drive is the machine for quality shoot-'em-ups. There are any number that could of featured in the Hall of Fame: CYNOUG, ZERO WING, SUPER FANTASY ZONE - but I picked this one, because it's the hardest.

8
PROJECT X
AMiGA

This game is so hard, if you lose your power-ups at the wrong moment you may as well go and do some gardening because you're as good as dead. Still, in an age when most games are ridiculously easy, I prefer them this way.

9
UN SQUADRON
SUPER NES

This wartime shoot-'em-up provides a nice bit of variation from the space-based shooters, providing that when it comes to arcade conversions - just give them to Mr Capcom and he'll do the business.

10
BiONiC COMMANDO
NES

Another creaky classic, this one has been out for about three years, but is still one of the best NES games around. As well as shooting people, you have a handy bionic arm which you can chuck out and use to swing from trees!

FEMALE RELATIVES ONLY
GAMESMASTER'S GRANNY GAMERS

It is sometimes claimed that video games are strictly for the young and foolish.

At GAMESMASTER, however, we came across three people that disprove the first part of the argument completely. The jury's still out on the matter of foolishness!

Letty Edwards, Barbara Jones, and Joan Thornley are games fanatics, but all of them are, shall we say, in the autumn of their years. These ladies remember things like trams, rationing and Labour governments.

There's no denying, however, that in their hearts they're still slips of girls, ready for anything and as keen to spend an evening with a firm grip on a joystick as any young male in the first flush of youth.

As a special GAMESMASTER treat, we decided to fill their handbags with change and pack them off to London's world famous TROCADERO and let them loose on the very latest arcade action.

First call was on the SUZUKA 8-HOUR RACING SIMS something to do with the attraction of STRADDLING ALL THAT THROBBING POWER. Many memories came flooding back to our gamers, though strangely none had ever ridden a motorbike before. Barbara proved particularly adept on her hog, winning most of the races.

Our intrepid trio then moved onto VIRTUAL REALITY, re-inacting LAWNMOWER MAN as Bathchair Women and enjoying every PERCEPTION-ALTERING second of it.

After the delicate VR maneuvering, Joan decided to show that her long spell as British Light Heavy-weight Champion in the '50s had not gone to waste as she unleashed some aggression on SONIC BLASTMAN.

Then, to round off the day, we thought we'd put the nerve of our Gaming Grannies to the ultimate test and invite them TO RIDE THE STOMACH-CHURNING R360. Letty stepped forward, strapped herself in and went for it. She emerged admitting to slight queeziness but with a verdict of 'SUPER', apparently Granny-speak for TOTALLY AWESOME.

AUNTIE MARISIA'S CHALLENGE

Regular viewers of the last series will remember when Auntie Marisia put down her fondue set and picked up a Neo-Geo joystick to have a go at winning 'a golden one', as we say in the trade. Now Auntie Marisia may look like a kind, sweet lovable woman, but there is a dark, violent, almost psychopathic streak in her, which was reflected in her choice of game: KING OF THE MONSTERS. She was playing against that most gregarious of gaming grannies, LETTIE EDWARDS. Marisia was playing as SUPER GRON a godzilla-type monster who's speciality was throwing opponents into the air, and impaling them on it's spiky back upon landing,

Anyway, it came to Round 2, and Lettie really had some work to do. Fortunately for her, she discovered her own special move, which enabled her robot fighter to launch missiles from his back. Auntie Marisia used the rather bizarre tactic of walking stright into these, a military move not seen since the Charge of the Light Brigade. So, Lettie took the second round, and her unstoppable momentum continued in the final round, and Auntie Marisia, sadly, got gubbed.

The two contenders emerged, bloddy from battle, but still retaining that inner beauty that only women 'of a certain age' have. Auntie was a good loser, not that she had any choice, and said that she 'likes a game she can get her teeth into' and that she had enjoyed this molar-tastic bout. Lettie walked away, Golden Joystick aloft, to get back to her daytime job as a karate instructor for the SAS. Hurrah!

infinitely more unpleasant than a night out in Swindon, if you ask me. Lettie opted for the robot fighter CYBER WOO, the kind of name that DEFINITELY gets you kicked in at school, and this was reflected in the first round, where Auntie gave Lettie a proper pasting.

AUNTIE MARISIA'S TOP TEN DELIGHTFUL DISHES

REVIEWED BY DOMINIK DIAMOND

OVER THE COURSE OF OUR STAY ON THE RIG, WE WERE SUBJECTED TO NUMEROUS SEAFOOD VARIATIONS FROM OUR 'CHEF DE CHEF' AUNTIE MARISIA. HERE ARE HER PERSONAL TEN FAVOURITES, WITH MY OWN TESTAMENT TO THEIR … ER … TESTEMENT-ABILITY.

1. DEEP FRIED HADDOCK IN A PIQUANT SHERRY SAUCE.
A LOT OF SO-CALLED COOKING EXPERTS HAVE AN ANCIENT PROVERB WHICH GOES 'SHERRY WITH FISH IS CRAP', BUT AUNTIE M PROVES THEM WRONG WITH THIS BEAUTY.

2. BABY CRABS, FRESHLY BOILED AND MASHED OVER A SEA OF GREEK LENTILS.
ONE FOR THE HEALTH FREAKS OUT THERE, ONLY $3^1/_2$ CALORIES PER MOUTHFUL, AND YOU DON'T REALLY WANT TO HAVE MUCH MORE THAN THAT.

3. LOBSTER THERMIDOR WITH RICOTTA CHEESE GRATIN.
AGAIN A SEEMINGLY IMPOSSIBLE DISH TO PULL OFF, BUT AUNTIE M LIKES TO DO THIS ON A SATURDAY, WHEN SHE HAS MORE TIME TO HERSELF.

4. FISH PIE SPECIAL.
WHEN AUNTIE FIRST STARTED OFFERING US HER FISHY PIE, WE TURNED OUR NOSES UP IN DISGUST, THE WHOLE AFFAIR SMELLED A BIT DODGY. BUT AFTER THE FIRST COUPLE OF MOUTHFULS, WE REALIZED IT TASTED VERY SUCCULENT.

5. KIPPERS IN FRESH ORANGE JUICE WITH CORNFLAKE CRUMBLE.
AUNTIE MARISIA HATES WASHING UP, ESPECIALLY IN THE MORNING. SO, SHE CAME UP WITH THIS 'ALL-IN-ONE' BREAKFAST WHICH TASTES LIKE HELL, BUT ONLY USES ONE BOWL.

6. PRAWN BALLS COATED IN RUM, SERVED WITH CRISPY NOODLES AND BISTO GRAVY.

7. JELLIED EELS WITH LYCHEE DUMPLINGS.
WHAT A TROPICAL LUXURY THIS DISH WAS - A GREAT FAVOURITE ON THE RIG.

8. BOILED TADPOLES IN A BASKET.

9. WINKLES IN WHALE SPUTUM SAUCE.
AUNTIE M'S REMEDY FOR SEASICKNESS - A CALMING CONCONCTION FOR A DELICATE CONSTITUTION.

10. SPRAT NIBBLES AND SPICY CAJUN DIP
A DEF CERT FOR TICKLING THE APPETITE

STAR RIGGERS ref: xp 937564

JOHNNY HERBERT

I like Johnny Herbert. He's young, he's slick, he's good-looking and he has impeccable personal hygiene. However, this was no guarantee that he'd do the business when his gearstick was replaced with a joystick. However, the young Formula One driver had a few advantages: Not only was he playing a driving game, but that game was LOTUS 3, and he is after all, a member of the Lotus Racing Team. Now, LOTUS 3 is one of the tougher racing games out there, and the challenge was on a special GAMESMASTER course for added toughness. Johnny had to get through three checkpoints. At the first one, he was down by a few seconds after a poor start, but by the second checkpoint he'd made good time and was only one second behind. Unfortunately, he took one turn a bit too wide, smacked barriers and passed the finish line just one second over the time limit! This was a great shame, as we had a lot of technical problems that day, and Johnny had to hang around in his overalls for ages. Did he complain? Not once, in fact we sat for ages having a right old laugh in a 'blokey' fashion. Respect is due.

GAMESPLAYING SKILLS ★★★★
PERSONAL NICENESS ★★★★★

KRISTIAN SCHMIDT

NEIGHBOURS stars, eh? EASY LIFE! Swanning around in the fierce Aussie sun, cooling out in the coffee shop, taking Bouncer for a frolic, you'd think they'd all be pampered girls' blouses. Well, they are. Only kidding, all the NEIGHBOURS stars we've had on the show have been top blokes and I spent ages with Kristian getting all the gossip from him. I was especially interested in finding out if he's ever actually had a fling with any of the cast members. He told me... but it would be unprofessional for me to let you know! Anyway, as well as being a beautiful person, Kristian was another tragic celeb who had his gamesplaying ineptness exposed by a laserdisc shooting game, this time it was SPACE PIRATES. This is probably the hardest of the laserdisc games and Kristian certainly made a meal of it, which was a shame, because I thought he was the tops.

GAMESPLAYING SKILLS ★
PERSONAL NICENESS ★★★★

STAR RIGGERS ref: xp 784566

TONY SLATTERY

This was a tricky challenge and I realized Tony did not stand much of a chance - Tony knew he had NO chance, so he decided he would just have a laugh. And boy, did we laugh! Tony was easily the funniest bloke we've had on the Show after Vic Reeves, and he was the only celeb cool enough to admit that he hated video games. He was playing the laserdisc shooting game WHO SHOT JOHNNY ROCK, which is very tough but, because it features the most excruciatingly awful actors, gave Tony a fine scope to display his range of comic brilliance. Even when the camera stopped, he found it difficult to stop being funny, a problem I have never had. He got further than I thought he would, progressing to the last showdown before he shot an innocent woman by mistake. Oh well, *c'est la vie!*

GAMESPLAYING SKILLS *
PERSONAL NICENESS ****

STAR RIGGERS ref: xp 348676

STAR RIGGERS ref: xp 675686

STEVE BACKLEY

The obvious worry when you have someone like Steve Backley on the show is 'this is a bloke who throws a spear a hundred metres, if he loses and gets annoyed, how far will he throw me?' So, as you can imagine, I was rooting for Mr Backley every step of the way. When he arrived I approached him cautiously as he is a huge bloke. But his face broke into a smile and I realized he was far too nice to throw young Scottish TV presenters off oil rigs. He'd brought along one of his javelins and I gingerly felt the tip, hoping I would not end up impaled on it. So, to the challenge. It was a javelin event, surprisingly enough, on SUMMER CHALLENGE on the PC. It was a case of 'bash the buttons then get the angle right'. His opponent, Simon Hadley was a professional games tester, so things did not look good for big Steve. Simon went first and easily broke the 90 metres mark. Steve's first throw was in the low 80s. His next was a monster... but his feet were over the line and it was a foul. For his final throw he tanked it along the runway but his angle was too high and he ended up a good eight metres behind Simon. I made a quip about his great rival Jan Zelezny and his eyes darkened, but I lived. Phew!

GAMESPLAYING SKILLS **½
PERSONAL NICENESS *****

GAMESMASTER'S CONSOLETATION ZONE
AMIGA™

Let me guess. No, guessing is for people who don't know the answer. So, let me tell you.

You are a meagre Amiga gamer and you are having problems completing some of your favourite games. Well, fear not young rascals, you are not alone in your inadequacies. It is only a genius like I who knows true loneliness.

On these pages you will find some rather pathetic and some decidedly brilliant answers to some of the questions that crop up with annoying regularity. Read them and become a better person...

1. 'On MONKEY ISLAND 2, how can I win the spitting competition?'

'Go to the bar, buy a blue drink and a yellow drink. Mix them together to make a green one. Drink this to make your phlegm thicker and then spit when you see the breeze disturbing the scarf around the waist of the woman in the audience.'

2. 'On JAMES POND 2: ROBOCOD, I've heard that there's a cheat for infinite lives. Can you tell me what it is?'

'From the start, go right and enter the first door that you come across. Once you're inside, go to your right and just after the second set of spikes you will see five objects. Collect them in the following order: Lips, Ice-cream, Violin, Earth, Snowman. The first letters of these spell the word 'LIVES' and you now have an infinite amount of them.'

3. 'On PINBALL FANTASIES, is there any way I can make the game last longer?'

'When the game is scrolling downwards to show you the table, quickly type in 'EXTRA BALLS' for, you've guessed it, extra balls. You should now be able to amass a truly whopping score.'

4. 'Are there any secret bonus areas on ZOOL?'

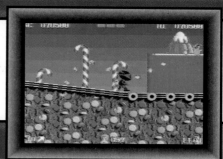

'There certainly are, in fact there is a special Gamesmaster bonus room in my honour. This is located on the third level of Sweet World. When you're on the level, let the clock run down to zero, then you can walk straight through the first right hand wall that you come to and you will reap the rewards.'

5. 'I'm finding THE ADDAMS FAMILY very difficult. I wonder if you have any tips to make it easier.'

'Try entering the password IIIII at the start of the game and you will begin with 100 lives.'

6. 'Can you help me find the hidden levels in FIRE AND ICE?'

'To reach the first secret level in Ice world you will have to pass through two warps. The first is to the far right of level 2 and can be reached by shooting invisible bonus blocks. Once you've been warped to the next level, walk right where you'll find a cane and another hidden bonus block. Simply jump onto the block and then into the air to reach the secret level.'

forty-five

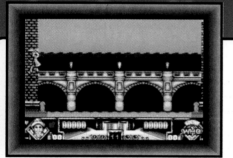

7. 'Where are the extra lives and weapons in DALEK ATTACK?'

'Run across the River Thames and climb to the top of the building you see on your left. When you reach the top, leap as far to the right as you can. Platform steps will miraculously appear beneath you. If you take seven more steps to the right and then jump, another platform will appear beneath you. Keep jumping left and right across the screen until you jump to collect the extra life and bonuses. This will triple the power of your sonic screwdriver and make it easier to destroy the ogre guarding the prison door.'

8. 'I'm having trouble with THE CHAOS ENGINE. What do you suggest?'

'Well, you could try being better at games, but if that fails, go to the password section and enter all Ts, all Vs, all Xs or all Ys. Level one will start to load but before it is done you will enter the shop with loads of lives. You will have loads of money with which to buy those lives and you can then go about the game more or less invincible.'

★★★
GAMESMASTER'S HALL OF GAME FAME
★★★

TOP TEN ALL-TiME GREATS

③ SEGA ViRTUA RACiNG

The nearest it gets to driving a racing car without having to fork out millions of quid and get oil all over your hands. The best bit is the seat, which squashes your bum as you go round a particularly tight corner.

① STREETFiGHTER 2 – CHAMPiONSHiP TURBO EDiTiON

An easy choice this. It's the most successful arcade game of all time and deservedly so. Inventive special moves, great characters and unbelievable speed make this the un-disputed king of beat-'em-ups.

② MORTAL KOMBAT

While this was never going to be better then STREETFiGHTER, the digitized film graphics and blood-curdlingly violent special moves make it better to look at, if not to play.

④ SUZUKA 8-HOUR MOTOR RACiNG

Standard bike racing game, rendered a bit special if you have seven mates to line up alongside you. Then it gets seriously com-petitive in a 'push friend off bike for a laugh' type situation.

ARCADE GAMES

⑤ TERMINATOR 2

The best film based arcade game ever. Simple to play - you have the machine gun in your hand and you blast everything that moves. The neat thing about this is how it closely relates to the film, and actually requires you to think a bit in the later levels.

⑥ LETHAL WEAPON 3 PINBALL

Pinball games are a wonderful invention, this one gets the vote because of the mini-video screen which has this great bit where you're in a fight and you push the flipper buttons as hard as you can to duff your opponent up. A bit irresponsible, but great fun!

⑦ SMASH TV

Gameshows of the future will require you to kill lots of mutants and androids to win toasters and cars, if this game is to be believed. Anything's better then BOB'S FULL HOUSE, especially this 'shoot everything that moves' affair.

⑧ SOCCER BRAWL

Soccer hard man Vinnie Jones played this on the Show, which was pretty apt, as it's a futuristic version of the traditional ball-kicking game with the ability to kick, punch and even shoot your opponents. Not recommended as a one-player game, but we've all got friends, no?

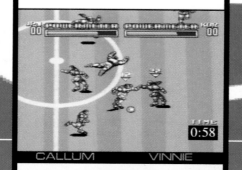

DEFENDER

⑨ DEFENDER

Ancient one this, but the forerunner of every space shoot-'em-up to date. You can still find it in older arcades, and it's well worth a try. There's about half a dozen buttons though, so get a mate to help you hyperspace!

⑩ EURO SOCCER CHAMP

Another football game which allows you to kick and punch the opposition and even the referee. The rather smart 'TV camera' style graphics which zoomed in close-up for things like fouls, victory celebrations make this game a jot different from the rest.

forty-seven

1. What was MARIO'S profession in the original design stages of the first Mario game?

A) Geography Teacher
B) Electrician
C) Carpenter

2. What is the name of SONIC'S enemy?

A) Dr Robotnik
B) Dr Death
C) Dr Legg from Eastenders

3. What was the name of the SPORTS SIM that spent more weeks at the TOP of the AMIGA chart than any other game in 1992?

A) Sensible Soccer
B) Sensible Football
C) Stupid Lacrosse

4. Where is ZOOL from?

A) Planet X
B) The Nth Dimension
C) Grimsby

5. JOHN MADDEN of JOHN MADDEN '93 fame is:

A) A Postman
B) A Golfer
C) An American Footballer

6. STARWING, the first SNES game to use SFX technology, was released under another name in the US. What was it?

A) Star Fox
B) Star Fighter
C) Clive

7. The top-programming team behind HITS like SPEEDBALL 2 and GODS is:

A) The Megabyte Brothers
B) The Bitmap Brothers
C) The Beverly Sisters

8. The excellent follow-up to DESERT STRIKE is called:

A) Air Strike
B) Jungle Strike
C) The Miners Strike

9. Amiga is Spanish for:

A) Girlfriend
B) Sexy
C) Better than the ST

10. The latest in a successful line of licensed FOOTBALL games from KRISALIS SOFTWARE is:

A) Chelsea: Not Even A Sniff Of A Major Trophy In The Last Twenty Years
B) AC Milan: Simply The Best
C) Manchester United: League Champions

11. The point of that two-and-a-half minute advert from Sega was to:

A) Sell some Mega CDs
B) Show-off
C) Who said anything about there being a point to it?

12. Road Rash is:

A) A top game by Ocean
B) A top game by Electronic Arts
C) A rather embarrassing complaint suffered by cyclists

13) What is the name of the COMPANY behind the revolutionary INTERACTIVE MULTIPLAYER technology?

A) 3Di
B) 3 Nelson Mandela
C) 3DO

14) ECCO is a :

A) Whale
B) Dolphin
C) Ecco is a... ecco is a...

ARE YOU A GAMESMASTER?

15) You are stuck in the fifth dimension of GOBLIN WORLD in Balrog: Master of Destiny and you cannot eat, sleep or talk until you escape. Should you:

A) Find the magical shamrock power-up in Sorcery Land to give you the strength to defeat the half-man, half-wardrobe end-of-level guardian, Eric

B) Use the mighty sword of Kudo to destroy the elf-like guardians of the valley of Shanber through which you can make your escape

C)   Get a life

16-20) From which games do the following screen shots come?

SCORING

Prepare yourself for the truth, you get one point for every correct answer.

HOW DID YOU SCORE

15-20: You're a GAMESMASTER, a SMARTY pants, a right BOFFIN, a gaming GURU, a Sega sage and a Nintendo know-it-all. Either that or you cheated. Either way, JOLLY WELL DONE.

10-15: NOT BAD. NOT GOOD, MIND, BUT NOT BAD. You know your way around games but a few more anti-social hours in front of that monitor are needed for the Power Up to true Gamesmastery.

Less than 10: Are you a PROFESSIONAL DIVVY? Did you go to divvy school, take divvy classes and graduate as head divvy? And do you now give divvy lessons at evening classes? You are completely CLUELESS when it comes to videogames and I can only suggest that you take up a more suitable hobby.

ANSWERS

1. C / 2. A / 3. A / 4. B / 5. C / 6. A / 7. B / 8. B / 9. A / 10. C / 11. A / 12. B / 13. C / 14. B / 15. C / 16. Jimmy White Snooker / 17. Cool Spot / 18. Muhammad Ali's Heavyweight Boxing / 19. Megalomania / 20. Superman

FANTASY CHALLENGES

You have no idea how frustrating it was on the Rig, having to hand over to the great Metal-Headed One week-in, week-out to dish out the Challenges, and did he ever ask for my opinion? Did he Swindon! It's all very well him saying 'Collect sixty squillion coins in SUPER MARIO WORLD'S Chocolate Island' and then have some kid come down and do it with one nano-second to spare, but IS THAT WHAT YOU, THE PUNTERS, REALLY WANT TO SEE? WELL, OK IT PROBABLY IS! But just imagine if I had my way, in a perfect world I would get the actual games characters themselves to take part in my own little fantasy challenges. Here are a few of them.

CHALLENGE 1
STREETFIGHTER 3 V MORTAL KOMBAT

This is the one game fans everywhere would sell their premium bonds to see. You get all the fighters from each game into their respective camps, I say 'Go!' and they all start kicking each other in. Just imagine, would DHALSIM'S fiery 'Yoga fire' breath be chilled out by an ice-blast from SUB-ZERO? And how would SONJA's scissor grab and slam do if the Babe of gaming Babe-Alonia CHUN LI was toe-tapping over her head? Wouldn't you like to see that cocky so-and-so GUILE combing his hair after a victory, only to have SCORPIAN throw his short spear with cord into his nancy green-vested abdomen.

THE OUTCOME
The competitors line-up against each other, then Eddie Honda says 'Do we really have to carry on fighting?' They all go off, arm-in-arm, to start a hippy commune in Thailand, making sandals out of raffia.

CHALLENGE 2
SUPER MARIO'S FACIAL HAIR CHALLENGE

We get the plumber himself on to the Show, and he has to play this game my programming mate Paul Ginger has concocted, called 'How to become a kids hero, in spite of having a really dodgy moustache'. Mario has ten years to go around the world, telling kids that being fat and having the kind of moustache your old uncle would be ashamed of is actually PRETTY COOL. Along the way he has to blast away any hedgehogs that get near him. There is a special trick on the last level, where Mario has to concede that his brother Luigi, is actually cooler than him. I think it'd be more puzzlingly addictive than LEMMINGS.

THE OUTCOME
Mario succeeds, the world falls under his bushy charms and everyone starts wearing horrible red dungarees. Mr Nintendo smiles proudly at his bank manager.

CHALLENGE 3
REAL LIFE SONIC THE HEDGEHOG

Sonic thinks he's SOOOOO cool, right? Whizzing around the green hill zone, bouncing on anybody that gets in his way. Let's see how he copes when he gets on the Show, eh? We will turn him into a REAL hedgehog, and place him in the middle of the M25, and see him speed his way through six lanes of traffic, trying to bounce off big monster 12-wheel trucks from Newcastle!

THE OUTCOME

Lots of monster 12-wheeled trucks from Newcastle with an attractive 'hedgehog' pattern on their tyres!

CHALLENGE 4
BLANKA GETS ON HIS BIKE

You can't be a Streetfighter for ever, and the day will come when Dramilian half-man/half-beast BLANKA will quit the fight game and have to get a proper job. We pre-empt that by getting him on the show to play an employment simulation game. Blanka has to successfully get a job as a merchant banker. It's a PLATFORM adventure, where he first of all has to find a barber willing to cut his unkempt hair. Then he has to find the right ingredients to make the soap in history that can get rid of his personal 'jungle' smell. This is followed by a two year Open University course in accountancy and finished with a driving course, where Blanka has to steer a Golf GTi through the City of London whilst talking into a mobile 'phone.

THE OUTCOME

Blanka's head explodes on Level One.

CHALLENGE 5
MODERN ROLE-PLAYING GAMES

We get all these role-playing blokes from every role-playing game that ever was with all their girly names like ORLOK THE WARRIOR and instead of placing them in the magical kingdom of XEEN where they have to find the sacred sceptre of Gobbledegook, we dump them in Glasgow, where they have to make their way from one end of the city to the other wearing Celtic scarves. The object is simply to survive. To make things even more difficult, every time they use stupid old-English language, like saying 'ye olde inne' instead of 'the old pub', they get ten health points taken off.

THE OUTCOME

The audience fall asleep, realizing this is, of course, the one challenge every series that we get completely wrong, and what we think will be an exciting televisual experience, turns our to be dealthy dull.

CHALLENGE 6
GRAHAM TAYLOR IS A LOSER

We get the England soccer manager Graham Taylor down to play SENSIBLE SOCCER ... against me! We both pick England, but my team consists of people like Chrissy Waddle, Peter Beardsley and Craig Maskell. We play open, attacking football, with passes along the ground and have players who will take on the opposition. He plays eleven players called CARLTON PALMER, lines them all along the goalmouth and says that 'every match at international level is a tough match'.

THE OUTCOME

I win 437-0, but Graham claims there was a lot of positive aspects to his team's performance, and that he considers it 'a moral victory'. And no, he won't resign, he's got a job to do, but he quite liked the look of that Chrissy Waddle who played for my team, but he'd never heard of him before.

NOT THE GAMESMASTER AWARDS

Each year there are numerous award ceremonies held in the world of video games. They range from those sponsored by magazines to those voted for by the heads of the gaming industry. The ceremonies are a good laugh, there's lots of free food, tizer and backslapping, but the awards they give out are for rather pointless reasons. Silly categories like 'BEST GRAPHICS', 'BEST SOUND' and 'BEST GAME' are not what it's all about really. In an age where family values are crumbling by the day, **I want awards that mean something.** So, we decided to have our own awards, and assembled a celebrity panel consisting of myself, Gamesmaster, Auntie Marisia and that grumpy bloke from ONE FOOT IN THE GRAVE. However none of them turned up, so I had to vote on my own.

COOLEST CHARACTER
DHALSIM (STREETFIGHTER 2)

SO laid-back the back of his head touches the ground when he walks, the Indian fighting master has all the essential ingredients needed to be cool: shaven head (very 'in' this year and cuts down on shampoo costs), lean body (it's not cool to be fat) and if he ever meets with a problem, he just levitates. Someone we all look up to.

RUNNER UP: SPOT (COOL SPOT) - tries a bit too hard. By calling yourself COOL you have a lot to live up to.

GRUMPIEST CHARACTER
RYU (STREETFIGHTER 2)

Does this bloke EVER smile? I mean, he's so full of it, even when he wins fights he looks like a wet Sunday in Woking - I bet if you went up behind him and tickled him while showing him Vic Reeves' video - the corners of his mouth would remain steadfastly down-turned.

RUNNER-UP: No one comes close to misery-guts above.

BEST EARS
SONIC THE HEDGEHOG

Ears are one of the most underrated ... er ... things that a video game character has. For this reason, many characters don't even have them, which I've never been too happy about. but by heck does SONIC have a pair on him! Big, flappy, blue and yet still aerodynamic. Marvellous.

RUNNER UP: MICKY MOUSE (WORLD OF ILLUSION) - Obvious, really.

WIMPIEST CHARACTER
First bad guy in STREETS OF RAGE 2

Just think how many times he's been kicked in by millions of people all over the world? What does he do? Nothing but come back for more. You could probably blow him over he's such a big girl's blouse.

RUNNER-UP: The second bad guy in STREETS OF RAGE 2.

THICKEST CHARACTER
PRINCESS DAISY from SUPER MARIO games

Ok, check this out. In each game, she's been kidnapped by BOWSER, or some similar nasty bloke. So Mario dons his moustache and rescues her, only for her to be kidnapped again in the very next game. Does she not realize she shouldn't talk to stangers, especially those who've kidnapped her before?

RUNNER-UP: ANY LEMMING - They're thick as well. Wandering off the side of cliffs and into flaming pits of lava. Sometimes I don't know what the world's coming to...

EASIEST GAME
TEENAGE MUTANT NINJA TURTLES: THE HYPERSTONE HEIST

If you're a bit rubbish on the old gamesplaying front then get this game, because if you keep doing flying kicks, you'll complete the whole thing in about half-an-hour. If you're good at games then ... er ... best avoid.

RUNNER-UP: the first version of SENSIBLE SOCCER.

HARDEST GAME
BATTLE SQUADRON - MEGADRIVE

I couldn't even get past the first level. This shoot-'em-up chucks everything at you, all at once, and multicoloured backgrounds make it difficult to make out the bad guys from the pretty floral scenery.

RUNNER-UP: SUPER PROTECTOR (SUPER NES) I cannot play this to save my life, I'm sorry, call me a big girl's blouse but I'm hopeless at it.

GAME CHARACTER I'D MOST LIKE TO BE STUCK IN A LIFT WITH
CHUN-LI (STREETFIGHTER 2)

Definitely the biggest babe in gaming history, the perfect mix of beauty and hardness. If we were stuck in a lift we could talk at length about oriental philosophy and hair-styling tips, and then she could do her 'flaming kick' to beak down the door and we wouldn't be trapped any longer. Hurrah!

RUNNER-UP: TOAD (SUPER MARIO WORLD) - Because he's so small, there would be tons of room for big, fat me.

HOME SWEET HOME

It's strange how attached you can get to the post-industrial hellholes we've called home. Now that the Church and the Rig have been atomized into the fifth dimension, Dominik thought he'd spend one idle afternoon staring out of the window, reliving his childhood fantasy of becoming an estate agent...

THE CHURCH

BUILT ....A couple of hundred years ago, maybe even more

SIZE ....100' x 80' (Main Worship Hall)
20' x 10' (Navel)
16' x 22' (Back Room)
12' x 12' (Square Room)
1000' x 10' (Long, Thin Room)
47' x 36' (Gamesmaster's Chamber)
10' x 8' (My Chamber)
2' x 1' (Monk's Chamber)

Plus numerous small dark rooms I was too timid to measure, and a large organ.

VIEW... A bit bleak I'm afraid, stuck in the middle of some dank misty moor or other. On a clear day you could see your toes.

FEATURES... Attractive masonry, beautiful cornices, and you should have seen the priest's hole - quite a sight. Regular congregation with hearty singing voices. Big bell. Roof in need of slight repair. 727 plug sockets.

THINGS TO DO... General worship and prayer. Tea dances. Choir practices. Raffles with daft prizes like old ties and home-made jam. Go for walks. Get lost. Get found again.

GOOD POINTS... Lovely atmosphere. Many candles. Peace and quiet

BAD POINTS... Freezing cold. Lousy television reception.

MARKET VALUE... Yours for a tenner. OK you have twisted my arm, let's make it £8.00 cash

BIZARRO'S ESTATE AGENTS SPECS.

THE RIG

BUILT .... Don't ask me, it wasn't my idea. Gamesmaster just got it into his head one day that we should start a holiday resort in the middle of the North Sea, where people could come out and visit to just play video games. I tried to humour him, next thing you know, I'm standing on deck, freezing to death!

SIZE .... 300' x 280' (Gamesplaying Area)
20' x 18' (Guests' Cabins x 200)
100' x 60' (Auntie Marisia's Kitchen)
God Only Knows How Big (Diver's Pit)
God Only Knows How Small (My Chamber)
7000' x 1' (A Big Pipe)
20' x 20' x 20' x 20' x 20' x 20' x 20' x 20' (Hexagonal Landing Pad used for Consoletation Zone)

VIEW .... Great if you like looking at water and seagulls.

FEATURES... Lots of pipes (ideal for the pipe enthusiasts amongst us); two cranes, a drilling derrick, a flare stack and private swimming pool (commonly referred to as THE SEA). Interesting internal architecture with unique 'dials' effect. Superb modern, pine-floored, fully-fitted kitchen, one of the largest of its kind and home to Auntie Marisia's little cooking experiments. (Cookbook not included, but that has never stopped Auntie Marisia - see page 41 for a selection of her best delicacies.)

THINGS TO DO... GREAT fishing, lots of fish to be caught, you can spend a relaxing afternoon fishing, and did I mention the great angling possibilities?

GOOD POINTS... Fresh air. Auntie Marisia's cooking.

BAD POINTS... Delivered pizza frequently cold. Can't nip down the shops for a loaf of bread and a packet of Opal Fruits.

MARKET VALUE... Priceless.

STAR RIGGERS ref: xp 679304

VIC REEVES

Without doubt the best fun I've had doing GAMESMASTER was when Vic Reeves paid a visit in conjunction with Comic Relief. He is the undisputed master of all things funny, and none of us were worthy to be in his presence. However, one thing you may not know about Mr Reeves is his fear of heights. When he got to the Rig, he took one look at the stairs and announced there was no way he would be able to walk down them. Now, because Vic is a comedian, we thought this was some kind of surreal joke, at which point we all fell about laughing at the sheer enormity of the man's wit. Then we realized he was serious, and he had a problem. What could we do? Would we break with tradition and have him coming up from the Diver's Pit? If he went down there, would he even return? As it was, Vic mustered his courage and came, slowly but surely, down the stairs, but was obviously still flustered when he played SLEEPWALKER, as he was so hopeless he got taken down to the Pit.

GAMESPLAYING SKILL *
PERSONAL NICENESS *****

CATHY DENNIS

Rock legend Cathy IS the Babe of Babe-Alonia as far as the boys in the GAMESMASTER office are concerned, and for some bizarre reason, the day she came down, everybody had their best clothes on, everyone had shaved and some of our researchers had EVEN washed to celebrate the occasion. Unfortunately, Cathy's gamesplaying skills did not quite match her niceness, as she failed most dismally on GLOBAL GLADIATORS. But we can forgive her that slightest of failings.

GAMESPLAYING SKILLS
Off the scale (dismal)
PERSONAL NICENESS
Off the scale (in the nicest way)

STAR RIGGERS ref: xp 362436

TAKE THAT

I'm not a massive fan of their records, but definitely one of the nicest bunch of blokes on the planet, 'The Thats' (as they are known in the business) put all thoughts of friendship aside as they fought each other on DYNABLASTER, the classic maze shoot-'em-up. The winner is the last one alive, and Gary and Mark quickly fell by the wayside, leaving Jason and Robbie fighting to the last. Robbie eventually won, much to my delight, as he had said beforehand he was a big fan of the show. Flattery gets you everywhere.

GAMESPLAYING SKILLS
* * (Gary/Mark)
* ****(Jason/Robbie)

PERSONAL NICENESS *****

STAR RIGGERS ref: xp 579606

'HACKSAW' JIM DUGGAN

A lot of people say WWF Wrestling is a big fake, well, I can assure you that 'Hacksaw' Jim Duggan is most certainly for real. No-one could pretend to be that manic which fitted in perfectly for our Show. Most of the time I told celebs what I would talk to them about when the cameras roll, but with the Hacksaw it was a case of just standing back and watching him go. I'm not that knowledgeable about the WWF, but from what I worked out, Jim Duggan is called 'Hacksaw' because he carries a lump of wood around with him, which is further proof that Americans will go for anything if someone tells them to. Hacksaw plucked a young contender from the Rig's audience then lived to regret it as the kid pulverized him on WWF on the Super Nintendo. Mr Duggan was then sent down to the Pit, but ended up carrying the Diver off, because that's how they do things in the wrestling world. Allegedly.

GAMESPLAYING SKILLS *
PERSONAL NICENESS ****

STAR RIGGERS ref: xp 045233

GAMESMASTER'S CRYSTAL BALL
HARDWARE: THE FUTURE

SEGA

The Mega CD; OK, it's pretty nifty, but it isn't exactly TOMORROW'S WORLD is it?

I mean, as a cutting edge it's going to have trouble slicing its way through butter. And, let's be honest, we might have all been pretty excited at first, but it hasn't exactly set the world on fire has it? It hasn't really singed the Isle of Wight.

But fret not Sonicophiles, Sega is aware of this little problemette and has already handed out the white coats, clip boards and nerdy specs to the people who work in the **'Cor, What a Great Idea' department and told them to come up with 'The Next Big Thing'.**

MEGA CD

Gamesmaster Intelligence (now there's a couple of words in the English language that don't sit comfortably together) reports that the boffin brigade has already made progress.

The next generation Sega console is, in fact, already completed. **It is CD based and is at least 32-bit. It is compatible with the Mega CD but may not have a cartridge port.** It even has a name; **Saturn.** At the moment, however, Sega says that it can't mass produce this beast for a reasonable price and so its launch is on hold. **Expect it in 1995 for around £399 and get ready to have your socks knocked off.**

In the meantime, prepare to have them at least rolled down a little bit by **Sega VR. This new audio/visual headset works in conjunction with your Mega Drive and is a step towards the world of Virtual Reality.**

It's not a giant step as the games will still be being played through a Mega Drive so don't expect any LAWNMOWER MAN type shenanigans.

Sega VR should be in the shops very soon for the Virtually Reasonable price of around £150-£200. It will come packaged with at least one game and Sega is working on more VR games to be sold separately.

ЛINTENDO

Nintendo is in no hurry to plunge into the brave new world of CD gaming. It is actually rather insistent that there is plenty of life left in the not-exactly-cowardly world of cartridges.

There have, however, been suggestions from harsher tongues than mine that the firm is taking a rather Luddite view of the emerging technology. (The Luddites are a little known, zealous but, nevertheless, sad pressure group from Kansas which insists that Betamax will end up as the dominant home video player format!)

But Nintendo insists that its attitude is formed out of fairness for its players rather than fear of the future. **It argues, it is concerned with the here and now** - not the somewhere over there, some time next year... possibly.

It's also gone on record as saying that it isn't interested in launching any hardware with a price tag higher than £200 and that the CD systems available for anything like that money don't offer any significant advantages over carts.

SNES - TODAY OR TOMORROW

The Japanese giant has decided that there is no point in launching a 16-bit bolt-on SNES CD drive as 32-bit is now the minimum requirement - and the days when a 32-bit CD system can be sold at Nintendo-type prices are definitely some way off.

So for now and for some time to come, the SNES is Nintendo's leading machine and the firm will concentrate on making its software better and better through enhancements like the SFX chip rather than chase the dream of CD.

3DO

Usually pronounced THREE-DEE-WHO?, these guys could actually represent the future of gaming.

OK, they haven't actually launched a machine yet and in fact, they don't ever plan to. Details, mere details.

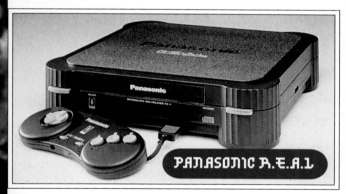

PANASONIC R.E.A.L

What 3DO have done is come up with a **technology, a new format which it is licensing to some of the biggest electronics manufacturers in the world.**

The firm was set-up by Trip Hawkins the man who established Electronic Arts, the biggest games publisher in the world. It's backed by companies like MCA/ UNIVERSAL, TIME WARNER, MATSUSHITA, AT&T and EA itself - more big names than the Polish phone book.

To attract that sort of backing, the 3DO technology would have to be pretty good. It is.

It's a CD format based around a 32-bit processor but has custom-built sound and graphics chips and can display and move images around 100 times faster than machines like the SNES or Mega Drive.

Its clarity of image is also rather stunning. Current systems can display around 256 colours. 3DO machines will offer a **mind-blowing 16 million colours.** Who knew there were 16 million colours??!

Early demos have had audiences agog. In fact some hardened industry veterans declared that they have never had such high expectations for a new format.

The first 3DO based machine will be launched by Panasonic and should be in the shops for summer 1994. It will come complete with a pretty hefty price tag of around £600-700, but the firm insists that the price will fall quickly and by 1995 a version could be on the market for the same sort of bucks as a Mega CD will set you back this Christmas.

So, **3DO; the future of games playing? Well, just possibly. And if it is, remember where you read it first.** If it isn't then this is the 1993 Blue Peter Annual signing off from somewhere beyond tomorrow.

fifty-nine

GAMESMASTER COMPETITION ACCESS ALL AREAS!

Win a VIP Trip to the Gamesmaster Set

Gamesmaster thrives on competition– it's what we're all about, whether it's one-on-one, head-to-head, against the clock or human type thing against the machine. So here's another competition, which will give three lucksome winners the chance to spend a day filming with GAMESMASTER, meeting the celebs, hanging out with the charismatic dudes who appear on your screens every week, popping up in the audience (and who knows being spotted by major Hollywood agents - not), and just generally getting under everybody's feet all day. It's generous, it's warm-hearted, yes - it's beyond the call of duty, but then that's the kind of guys we are.

All you have to do is **answer the three extraordinarily simple questions below, complete the tie-break** and stick it all on the most ridiculous postcard you can find to

GAMESMASTER COMPETITION
Virgin Publishing
PO Box 1870
London W10 5ZJ

so it arrives no later than 1st March 1994. You must give your **name, address, phone number and age.**

Here we go:

1
In what sort of building did the first ever series of Gamesmaster take place?

2
Which relative of Dominik Diamond is famed for her cooking?

3
Which soccer star was unbeatable on STRIKER?

TIE BREAK
In not more than 15 words complete the following sentence:

I think I'm made of the right stuff for Gamesmaster because ....

Don't hang around - send your postcard off today, and you might, just might, be part of the next GAMESMASTER series.

RULES

1. All instructions form part of the rules, and entry into the competition confirms acceptance of those rules.

2. This competition is open to all residents of the UK and Ireland except employees of Virgin Publishing Limited, Hewland International, Channel Four Television, their agents, suppliers, distributors and retailers (and their immediate family).

3. The entry is void if the postcard entered does not contain answers to all three questions and tie-break, name, address, phone number and age. Only one entry per person.

4. All entries become the property of Virgin Publishing Limited, whose decision is final in all matters; correspondence concerning results cannot be entered into.

5. A list of prize winners will be available after 1st March 1994 on receipt of a stamped, self-addressed envelope from: Gamesmaster Winners, Virgin Publishing, PO Box 1870, London W10 5ZJ.

6. All entries must be received no later than 1st March 1994.

7. The prize includes return travel from home to the Gamesmaster set for each winner and guardian (where winner is under 16).